# Black in White

# The girl from Niue

*and other poems from the*
*Black in White Poetry Competition 2024*

## CHARLOTTE SHYLLON
+ 29 contributing poets

© Charlotte Shyllon, 2024

First published in 2024 by Paragon Publishing, Rothersthorpe

Cover design: Christine Welby www.1stimpression.org

Front cover illustration: Tia Diana Draws IG: @tiadianadraws

Images used under license from Shutterstock.com

www.blackinwhiteservices.co.uk

The rights of Charlotte Shyllon to be identified as the author of this work have been asserted by her in accordance with the Copyright, Designs and Patents Act of 1988.

The author of each poem included retains the copyright for their individual poems.

All rights reserved; no part of this publication may be reproduced, stored in a retrieval system, or transmitted in any form or by any means, electronic, mechanical, including scanning, photocopying, recording or otherwise without the prior written consent of the publisher or a licence permitting copying in the UK issued by the Copyright Licensing Agency Ltd.
www.cla.co.uk

*Transforming Words Ltd.* trading as *Black in White*

ISBN 978-1-78792-073-6

Book design, layout and production management by Into Print
www.intoprint.net
+44 (0)1604 832149

# CONTENTS

Dedication and Acknowledgements . . . . . . . . . . . . . . . . . . . . . . . . . . 6
Foreword . . . . . . . . . . . . . . . . . . . . . . . . . . . . . . . . . . . . . . . . . . . . . . . 7
Introduction. . . . . . . . . . . . . . . . . . . . . . . . . . . . . . . . . . . . . . . . . . . . . 9

## SECTION 1: Black in White Poetry Competition 2024 . . . . . . 13

- Sharing poems, opening minds      15
- Meet the judges      16
- How and why the winners are chosen      18

## SECTION 2: Poems by Charlotte Shyllon . . . . . . . . . . . . . . 21

- RACISM IS WRONG      25
- Alone. Again. Yet I abide      27
- Believe in you      31
- She tried to root out a dentist and failed      35
- We're in Saint Lucia, aren't we?      39
- Stop lumping us all together      43

## SECTION 3: Guest Poets' Poems . . . . . . . . . . . . . . . . 45

- "I'm a new hire…" – PoetryGirl4.0      47
- Thief or cleaner, cleaner or thief? – PoetryGirl4.0      51
- Give us our country back… – PoetryGirl4.0      55
- Filters – Serena Malcolm      59
- In the silence that is my right – Rick Dove      63

## SECTION 4: Winning Poems 2024 – Workplace Category.. .. 65

- 1st prize: The girl from Niue: Lunchbreak at Pegworth Plastics – John Gallas     67
- 2nd prize: Not one of us! – Chantel Ndubuka     69
- 3rd prize: Unheard – Andre Le Coz     73

## SECTION 5: Winning Poems 2024 – Childhood Category .. .. 75

- 1st prize: The reason I punched Gary – Emma Conally-Barklem     77
- 2nd prize: My skin is made of earth – Gwyn Yvere     81
- 3rd prize: A puppet of your parents – Yohana Gasu     83

## SECTION 6: Highly Commended Poems 2024 (in alphabetical order).. .. .. .. .. .. .. .. .. 85

- A case of mistaken identity? – Yvette Beckley [Workplace]     86
- A journey through judgement – Jamal Adewunmi [Childhood]     87
- An educated Black man signing on in 21st century Britain – Dr G [Workplace]     89
- Being a woman of colour in policing – Saara Nawaz [Workplace]     91
- Between the rock and the wall – Carole Greco [Childhood]     93
- Black girl, white world – Karenne Small [Childhood]     95
- But have *you* ever experienced racism? – Neelam Sharma [Childhood]     97
- Dark Cinderella – Cristina Akos Obazee [Workplace]     99
- Ifs, buts, and maybes – Anu Kehinde [Workplace]     100
- Interviewing whilst black – Dr G [Workplace]     103
- Invisible chains on me – Paarth Aggarwal [Workplace]     105
- Mission – Mike Dixon [Workplace]     106
- Natural selection – Izabella Osijo [Childhood]     107
- Small wound – Isaura Barbé-Brown [Workplace]     109
- So why aren't we pleased by the token Black poet? – Ross Clarke [Childhood]     111
- Still living – Mbeke Waseme [Childhood]     112
- Take it where?! – Niam Moore [Workplace]     115
- They know too – Nicole Kasumu [Childhood]     119

- True colours – JoshuaF [Childhood]     121
- What's in a name? – Eltayeb Bashar [Childhood]     122
- Who am I? – Theone Ampofo [Childhood]     124

## SECTION 7: About Black in White .. .. .. .. .. .. .. .. .. .. .. .127

- About us     129
- Our products     129
- Our services     130
- Our team     130
- Contact us     131

## Dedication

This book, like its predecessors, is dedicated to all those who see and value the benefits of equity, diversity and inclusion, and who labour actively in whatever capacity within this field to help open the minds of those who are the reason why these poems have been written…

## Acknowledgements

I would like to acknowledge several people who have been instrumental in helping me compile the contents for this book.

- All the poetry competition entrants, especially those featured in this book. Without their poems, this book wouldn't be as content rich as it is. Not everyone could be selected and celebrated publicly, but I appreciate everyone's efforts.
- My fellow judges in the Black in White Poetry Competition who diligently undertook an iterative judging process to select the winning and highly commended poems.
- The members of the Black in White team who are committed to our common passion project, and most of whom contributed this year to the initial shortlisting of all the poems we received.
- My partner Bernard, my children Andrew and Olivia, and all my other family and friends who gave an encouraging word or two along the way or who provided support and inspiration.

Most of all, I thank God for giving me the passion, strength and focus to continue on this journey.

# FOREWORD

Witnessing the rise of the 'far-right', many of us consoled ourselves that *'it couldn't happen here'*. Surely not in a multi-cultural United Kingdom, formerly with a global reputation for fairness and tolerance. Increasing anti-migrant, post-Brexit rhetoric and government policies contravened both international laws and common decency. Nevertheless, most UK citizens have been appalled by the nature and scale of atrocious violence that recently engulfed many cities across the country. More positively, many have countered the violence with acts of solidarity; refusing to draw lines in communities based on skin colour, culture, or religion that aim to discriminate *'us'* from *'them'* and *'I'* from *'you'*.

Irene Claremont de Castillejo, a Jungian analyst, was once asked whether she found listening and talking to clients taxing. Irene reflected that what exhausts us is division and lack of connection with others. Research confirms this – social isolation is bad for people's mental and physical health and wellbeing. So are racism and discrimination, which are inextricably linked to structural inequalities. During the pandemic, we saw how some people's intersectional identities increased their risk of chronic illness; sub-optimal healthcare ultimately meant they were most likely to die from COVID-19. Irene advocates opening our ears; I suggest we should 'listen with our hearts' to counter dehumanisation and truly connect beyond the words.

Poetry affords us ways to meet 'the other', those with whom we seem to have little in common, and find resonance. A subtle, courageous, and rebellious art form, poetry is powerful. Poetry changes you, touches you, and makes you feel your humanness. By the exactness of its words, powerful images may be conjured up and conveyed in a few lines that don't even need to rhyme! Sometimes poetry's power and impact emanate from the spaces between the words. Silence can and often does speak far louder than, for example, the shouting of racial slurs, threats, and incitement to violence recently seen across Europe and North America in particular.

Charlotte, thanks for inviting me to contribute to this important and timely work. Reading this anthology has been a moving experience, especially in the contemporary socio-political climate. Sincere thanks also to the authors for sharing your hearts and creativity with the world. In doing so, you have inspired me to redouble my personal commitment to tackling health inequalities, particularly at the intersections with 'race', gender, and socio-economic status. Evidence of ongoing racial disparities highlight the need to focus on legacy building to 'pass the baton' to future generations of researchers, practitioners and policy makers.

**Dr Dawn Edge**
*Professor of Mental Health & Inclusivity and Academic Lead for 'Race',*
*Religion & Belief, The University of Manchester*
*Director, Equality, Diversity & Inclusion Research Unit (EDI-RU),*
*Greater Manchester Mental Health NHS Foundation NHS Trust*

# INTRODUCTION

## Harnessing the power of words to transform hearts, minds and lives

If you have been following the Black in White journey, you know that I am a huge proponent of poetry. It is an aesthetic medium of expression and it is a creative art form that I embraced as a hobby more than eight years ago. I find the process of crafting poems stimulating and cathartic. Poems can be personal and intimate. They can help the reader to contemplate the messages being conveyed thoughtfully and to consider their own feelings about them.

Poetry is an engaging means of sharing powerful content; it can pack a punch. It has been used to great effect by many brilliant poets throughout the centuries to deliver some uncomfortable but salient messages. I have used poems to narrate some of my experiences of racism and unconscious bias in the workplace and in childhood, to provide insight and illumination on some of these issues. The power of poetry is that people consume and respond to it in a way that is personal to them, and this can make it very impactful.

Four years ago we started the Black in White Poetry Competition to give other people a platform for sharing some of their experiences and observations on racism. The trigger for this was the killing of George Floyd. Since then, we have seen time and time again why we must continue to share our voices.

Following the riots and protests that occurred across the UK earlier this year, the Chief Executive Officer of Amnesty International UK said "The widespread violence and hate crimes we've seen over the last few days are unacceptable". She called on the Government to "address the root causes of racism, Islamophobia and xenophobia that plague our cociety. It remains to be seen how they do this.

In the meantime, those of us operating at the grassroots must and will continue to do what we can to help transform hearts, minds and lives.

## Introducing The Transforming Words Foundation

Eight years ago when I set up a communications consultancy, I decided to call it Transforming Words. This is because I have always loved writing – both prose and poetry – and firmly believe that when words are carefully crafted into compelling content, they can be truly transformative.

Eight years down the line, we have now established a charity called The Transforming Words Foundation. The Black in White team transitioned into the Foundation over the last few months, and the soft-launch of the charity coincided with the launch of this anthology. The charity has been set up to continue and extend the work that we began via Black in White four years ago.

The Transforming Words Foundation's vision is:

> *A world where every voice is heard, understood, and valued through the transformative power of words. We envision a future where creative expression is accessible to all, bridging divides, promoting healing, and fostering a global culture of empathy and inclusion.*

Its mission is:

> *To create safe spaces where writing serves as a powerful tool for healing, resilience, and social change. We empower individuals to confront and express experiences with racism, prejudice, and personal challenges through the transformative power of words. By using poetry and prose, we illuminate the impact of racism, celebrate all forms of diversity, and inspire the transformation of minds, hearts, and lives.*

The Black in White poetry competition will continue as a key programme under the auspices of The Transforming Words Foundation. Additionally, we will initiate several new workstreams and programmes which will aim to address racism using words. We will add activities that showcase the value of embracing differences and understanding how equity, equality, diversity, inclusion and belonging can enhance all aspects of society.

## What's next for The Transforming Words Foundation?

We have created our strategic and operational plans and are starting to apply for the grants and funding that will allow us to initiate our programmes.

Our intention is that The Transforming Words Foundation will become a registered charity, pending acceptance of our application to become a charitable incorporated organisation (CIO) by the Charity Commission.

We are honoured to have four upstanding individuals who have come on board as our founding Trustees to provide strategic oversight. They are:

- **Annette Fisher:** an award winning architect of Nigerian descent, managing partner of her own firm FA Global, founder and co-chair of Unionne, chair of Let's Build and a published author.
- **Tanya von Ahlefeldt:** a senior healthcare communications consultant, who is also a specialist in diversity, equity, inclusion and belonging, and the god-daughter of the late Nelson Mandela.
- **Keith Aki-Sawyerr:** an experienced engineer who has made the transition to strategic leadership and management.
- **Dean McCarthy:** a seasoned family lawyer working with Charles Allotey & Co Solicitors.

We look forward to building a successful Foundation by continuing to use the power of words to bring transformation to individuals and societies.

*Charlotte Shyllon,*
*Founder and Chief Executive Officer,*
*The Transforming Words Foundation*

## Quotable Quotes

"Where, after all, do universal human rights begin? In small places, close to home."

*Eleanor Roosevelt*

# SECTION 1:

# Black in White Poetry Competition 2024

# Black in White
# Poetry Competition
## 2024

Have you experienced racism, prejudice, unconscious bias or microaggressions as a child or as a working adult?

Write about your experiences in a poem and enter this year's Poetry Competition. Your poem could help bring insight and illumination to the race-related issues that many people of colour experience, to build understanding and drive change.

This year's categories:
**1. Workplace racism · 2. Childhood racism**

You could win one of our top cash prizes per category:

**1st prize £250**

**2nd prize £125**

**3rd prize £75**

The winning poems and around 25 highly commended entries will be published in a new Black in White book, to be launched in October during Black History Month, and the contributors will receive a complimentary copy.

To enter:
1. Log onto www.blackinwhiteservices.co.uk/store, pay £1.50 per poem and obtain a payment reference*
2. Send your entry as a Word attachment by email to competition@blackinwhiteservices.co.uk, quoting your payment reference

## Don't delay, get writing today!

*Under 18 enter free. Poems must be your own work, previously unpublished, any style and any length. You can submit as many poems as you want. Poems are judged anonymously, so please do not include your name on the attachments. Full competition rules available at www.blackinwhiteservices.co.uk/poetry-competition-about-rules.

Closing date: Friday 21st June 2024

Black in White
www.blackinwhiteservices.co.uk

# About the Poetry Competition

## Sharing poems, opening minds

### Background

The Black in White Poetry Competition is an annual fixture on the calendar, launched every year on 21 March, which is World Poetry Day and International Day for the Elimination of Racial Discrimination. It gives people of all races, ethnicities and cultures an opportunity to share some of their experiences of and/or observations on racism in their own voices. It has been running for four years now. The first competition was open for entries in July 2021. The judging panel selected the winning and highly commended poems; we announced the results in September and two months later launched an anthology titled *Black in White Community Collection* (since retitled *Foreign body*).

In 2022 and 2023, we extended the entry categories to two – workplace and childhood – doubling the number of prizes from three to six. The resulting anthologies, *Black in White Community Collection Volume 2* (retitled *Here is your heart*) and *Her locks unveiled*, were launched during the UK's Black History Month celebrations in October. The new naming convention has been designed to ensure each anthology has a distinct identity.

The title of this year's anthology, *The girl from Niue*, is based on the title of the winning poem in the workplace category.

### This year's entries

The poems submitted into the 2024 poetry competition were superb. We received lots of entries from the UK and several other countries around the world. They told tales ranging from hurtful to hopeful. A veritable treasure trove of insights, illumination and inspiration! They were penned by people describing historical situations right up to the present day. They were written by those directly involved, those with views or observations on racism, and those commenting on stories in the media. They were submitted by children as young as 11 years old to older adults.

### Shout out to everyone

There were some excellent poems that didn't make it into this book purely because that's the nature of competitions. The judges would like to thank everyone for their entries and encourage all of those not included to keep telling your stories. Your voice is valued, respected and important.

## Meet the Judges

The five judges who reviewed, scored and selected the winning and highly commended poems this year were:

**Charlotte Shyllon** is the Founder & CEO of Black in White, established in 2020 and which was nominated for a 2024 National Diversity Award. She is the lead author of all of the Black in White anthologies. In 2023 her poem 'What if diseases didn't destroy destinies?' was selected for display at the Battersea Art's Centre and was one of 30 that inspired the People's Poem written by award-winning poet Jaspreet Kaur.

### Workplace category judges:

**Rick Dove** is a progressive poet and activist from South London. Published in literary anthologies, zines, and journals since 2016, Rick also has two solo collections with Burning Eye Books; Tales From the Other Box (2020), Supervillain Origin Story (2023), and was crowned UK Poetry Slam Champion in 2021.

**Akiebel Grant** is HR Manager at Police Now, working towards recruiting and developing frontline police officers and detectives that represent the communities they serve. She worked at the House of Lords for over 7 years, collaborating with the Diversity & Inclusion team. She led on initiatives such as a work experience scheme for people with learning disabilities, in partnership with Mencap, and was nominated for and won several awards.

# About the Poetry Competition

## Childhood category judges:

**Serlina Boyd** is the multiple-award winning founder of Cocoa, the UK's first Black children's magazines (Cocoa Girl and Cocoa Boy) established in 2020 to build her then 6-year old daughter's confidence after she was bullied at school because of her skin colour. The magazine is now sold globally, is in all UK schools and has an audience of 2.1 million. Serlina also set up the Cocoa Dream charity to help children increase their literacy skills.

**Jess Neil**, CEO of The Stephen Lawrence Day Foundation, is a proud intersectional feminist and anti-racist leader, with a passion for empowering socially ambitious organisations to align their actions with their core purpose. Drawing upon her rich experience of leadership, Jess works with her team to inspire change, advocate for social justice, and inspire a more equitable society for young people in Stephen's memory.

## How and why the winners are chosen

### The judging process

Every year we follow a rigorous judging process. We convene a judging panel for both categories to review and score the poems. We bring new judges on board every year; some are poets themselves, some from other backgrounds. The mix of perspectives makes for a well-rounded and inclusive approach.

This year, we included an extra shortlisting stage within the process because we received almost double the number of entries we have received in previous years. This was carried out by four members of the Black in White team: Hanna, Debbie, Jackie and Serena. The shortlisted entries were then sent to the judges, who reviewed all the entries anonymously.

Judging involves a detailed initial sift and first round scoring of the shortlisted poems by each of the judges individually against six criteria: 1) beauty, power, education or entertainment; 2) technical excellence; 3) form and flow; 4) choice of words and readability; 5) polish and expertise; and 6) overall impact.

The judges' individual scores are summarised and the poems listed in order based on the total scores they receive. The judges then review and discuss this allocation in a final judging session to ensure that the winning and highly commended selections exemplify the competition's objectives. We select the $1^{st}$, $2^{nd}$ and $3^{rd}$ placed winners in both categories, and up to 25 poems as highly commended.

We choose our winners in both categories from the rich repository of rhymes received with difficulty! The two final judging sessions last 90 minutes and we make good use of every minute. The highly commended entries are included primarily based on their scores and the judges' comments from the first round review. We then carefully consider and align on our choice of the top three poems in the two categories.

# About the Poetry Competition

## Our winners: Workplace category

❖ **1ST PRIZE**

**The girl from Niue: Lunchbreak at Pegworth Plastics by John Gallas**

This poem is short but impactful! It speaks to the fact that so many people still have misperceptions about how native people or indigenous tribes live in countries all over the world – in this case in Niue, a self-governing island state in the South Pacific Ocean, that's part of New Zealand. The poem describes how a girl from Niue handles her work colleagues' 'banter' during a lunch break by feeding into their ignorance. The judges all loved this poem. Our comments included: "Short, but impactful… I liked the short sharp sarcastic answers", "Says so much without being obvious – great!", and "Brought a smile".

❖ **2ND PRIZE**

**Not one of us! by Chantel Ndubuka**

This poem clearly describes how overt discrimination and unconscious bias can result in people who are different feeling or being excluded. It's about how a Black teacher's experiences at a new school eventually led to her departure – despite her efforts to stand firm – because at every step it was made clear to her that she wasn't accepted. The judges liked the use of repetition in the poem; one judge commented: "I felt the writer's pain. The final line in each verse being the same is impactful".

❖ **3rd prize**

**Unheard by Andre Le Coz**

As we know, the burden of historical mistreatments can impact people of colour at school and in the workplace. This poem starts here and expands into how never-ending these impacts can be; as one judge said: "This captures so much of the marginalisation in the workplace very well". The judges liked the fact that the poem highlights how people can be successful in the workplace despite these impacts by remaining (inwardly) defiant and standing strong.

## Our Winners: Childhood category

❖ 1ST PRIZE

**The reason I punched Gary by Emma Conally-Barklem**

With this poem, we get a powerful insight into what gave rise to a child's violent reaction to being verbally threatened with rape by another child who also called her the N word. Taught by her dad at age 7 to defend herself when required, she applies a punch that punishes Gary and gets her punished by her school. The judges were impressed and commented: "Wow! Beautiful, powerful, completely transported me... loved every word!" and "So rich! I like the style and use of language".

❖ 2ND PRIZE

**My skin is made of earth by Gwyn Yvere**

This poem speaks to the prejudice that starts in childhood, often learned from those who have the most influence over a young child – their parents. The judges said: "Really like this. Powerful expression of learned prejudice expressed and seeded" and "I really enjoyed this... it was very impactful".

❖ 3RD PRIZE

**A puppet of your parents by Yohana Gasu**

Again, this poem highlights the influence parents have on their children and how children are puppets who play out what their parents have taught them. Comments from the judges were: "A powerful, questioning look at how 'racism' results from puppeting not proper parenting, contrasted by the use of the word darling" and "A lovely poem, with a clear message"

## ✯✯✯ Well done to all of our winners! ✯✯✯

# SECTION 2:

# Poems by Charlotte Shyllon

The inspiration and context for each of the six new poems I have written for this book are described below:

- ❖ **RACISM IS WRONG:** The rationale for writing this poem is simple. I wanted to write an acrostic poem that spells out why racism is wrong – so it made sense to make this the title of the poem. Like many of my non-narrative poems, it states the problem and outlines the solution, seeking to solicit greater understanding and acceptance.

- ❖ **Alone. Again. Yet I abide:** According to the Office for National Statistics, the number of people in England and Wales who identified themselves as "Black, Black British, Black Welsh, Caribbean or African: African" in the 2021 census was 1.5 million or 2.5% of the total population. Around some conurbations, this percentage is higher of course. But I guess I shouldn't be too surprised when I walk into a room, especially in a corporate setting, and I am the only Black person present. Yet, it can be hard when no one else looks like me in meetings. This poem describes some of those impacts.

- ❖ **Believe in you:** A strong sense of self-belief can help anyone to succeed. But sometimes when you face discrimination because of somethings that's fundamental to who you are – your skin colour – it can shake you to your core because it's something you can't change. But you can't let it. You need to stand firm and believe in you. This poem explains why.

- ❖ **She tried to root out a dentist and failed:** This poem relates a true story that happened to a friend. Its focus is on colourism and prejudice, all forms of discrimination that we need to expose and eliminate. Thankfully, sometimes 'the system' can be relied upon to uphold justice, as in this case.

❖ **We're in Saint Lucia, aren't we?:** On a family trip to this beautiful Caribbean island, we were surprised to observe that the images on the walls of our hotel rooms were of White people. I've never been in a hotel room in a European country where the artwork in the rooms features Black people. This poem explains why I believe hotels should either be neutral or reflect the local population.

❖ **Stop lumping us all together:** Various terms that are used to describe people of colour collectively are falling out of favour – with good reason. We need to consider that groups called minorities in some societies are actually the Global Majority when viewed as a whole…

**Black in White**

# RACISM IS WRONG

*By Charlotte Shyllon*

| | |
|---|---|
| R | Racists think they are superior |
| A | And other races are inferior |
| C | Challenge their beliefs through education |
| I | Influence change through conversation |
| S | State the case for equality for all |
| M | Make this your constant clarion call |
| | |
| I | Insist on diversity and inclusion |
| S | Speak out against hate and exclusion |
| | |
| W | Write wise words, counter stinking thinking |
| R | Right the wrongs, be unshrinking |
| O | Open minds that are mistaken or misshapen |
| N | Negate negativity, be unshaken |
| G | Generate positivity, reawaken! |

## Black in White

# Poems by Charlotte Shyllon

## ALONE. AGAIN. YET I ABIDE.

*By Charlotte Shyllon*

I'm the lone Black face in the room, yet again.
I should be used to it, but no; so I count to ten.
It's 2024, things should be better by now.
But no. So I sigh, and I wonder when and how
Things will change. I want to feel relaxed
Instead of always feeling so taxed.

Other Black people in my profession
Have scaled the ranks, avoided suppression.
But we're tokens, few and far between.
While some lay low and are rarely seen,
Others are visible, symbols of diversity,
Doing what it takes to avoid adversity.

Sometimes, if I'm lucky, I may spot an ally
Someone who has my back, and who will try
To bring me in, not leave me out,
Whose words will leave no one in doubt
That even if I'm marginalised by some of the others
They'll speak up for me, when no one else bothers.

But often I'm in there on my own,
Female, Black, senior, and all alone.
Alone is a lonely place to be;
It can be hard when no one else looks like me.
Trying to strike the right balance, to be bold.

Strong enough to hold my own, and not be told.
To be assertive, not aggressive,
And certainly not to be suppressive.

Sometimes, if I've tried to take being alone in my stride
But failed, I've bailed.
Sometimes I feel fried, I've even cried.
But when I've dried my tears, I still my fears.
I reflect on my journey with pride –
The highs outweigh the lows, so I abide.

## Quotable Quotes

"When people get used to preferential treatment, equal treatment seems like discrimination."

*Thomas Sowell*

**Black in White**

## BELIEVE IN YOU

*By Charlotte Shyllon*

Believe in you,
Don't believe the lie;
The lie that says your hue
Means success will pass you by.
If someone says, 'Don't aim so high'
Don't believe the lie they spew.

I used to believe in me,
Because that's how I was raised.
But I imbibed the lie and I couldn't see
How someone like me could be praised;
It seemed much more likely I'd be erased
Since the lie made me feel confined, not free.

When you believe the lie
It can take you off your track;
When you believe the lie
The pressure may make you crack;
When you believe the lie
You may always feel you lack;
When you believe the lie
You may wish you were not Black.

**Black in White**

Dark skin shouldn't be a barrier to progress
So don't believe you're lower or less.
Know those who try to bring you down
Just because your skin is black or brown
Are ignorant, misinformed or biased
And need to be educated to the highest.

It took years for me to realise and repent,
To recall what my parents had instilled in me
To remember that if I believed and followed its scent
Sweet success could be mine, if I wanted it to be.
So I chose to forget about the years I'd misspent
Believing the lie, instead of believing in me.

When you believe in you
You won't care that your skin is dark;
When you believe in you
You can aim to make your mark;
When you believe in you
You can be as happy as a lark;
When you believe in you
You can knock it out of the park.

So, always believe in you.
Don't believe the lie.
You're more than just a colour or hue;
Take control and always try
To do your best, despite someone else's view.
Keep believing in you,
Keep reaching for the sky.

## Quotable Quotes

"Equality is leaving the door open for anyone who has the means to approach it; equity is ensuring there is a pathway to that door for those who need it."

*Caroline Belden*

# Black in White

## SHE TRIED TO ROOT OUT A DENTIST – AND FAILED

*By Charlotte Shyllon*

THE DENTIST
She'd graduated in dentistry
nearly 30 years previously,
the only black student in her year
and one of only a few at the uni.
She'd worked in the profession
and was known to be a good dentist –
highly respected by colleagues
and liked by her patients.
Raised to believe she could succeed,
she knew her value and never felt less.
She'd thrived over the years, until that day
when what happened shook her to her core.

THE PATIENT
She called the dental practice in pain
needing emergency attention.
The receptionist gave her an appointment –
not with her usual dentist,
but she took the slot anyway.
She arrived for her appointment
and sat in the waiting room.
When the dentist called her in
she was taken aback;
she'd thought a dentist with an English name
would be White, not Black!
She had no choice but to grin and bear it.

*THE COMPLAINT*
A few days later, she called back
saying she was in pain… again.
The emergency filling had fallen out,
and she blamed the dentist.
She called her incompetent
and said she had written to NHS England
questioning her qualifications and
asking them to check her practice procedures.
Angrily, she demanded a refund and
insisted they book her in with her usual dentist.
He looked like her – Asian like she was,
not a darker person.

*THE OUTCOME*
The practice stood by the dentist
They knew her to be highly professional
When NHS England reached out
She sent them her notes from the session
and awaited their response.
When they reported back
Their findings were indisputable:
"These notes are of a high standard
and the dentist showed empathy
When dealing with this patient."
Quashed, the patient withdrew her demand for a refund.
Chuffed, the dentist basked in her brownie points.

*THE LEARNINGS*
Call it what you will –
racism, discrimination, colourism,
prejudice, bias… unconscious or not.
Whatever. They're all wrong.
Put them aside.
See past someone's exterior;
what matters is the interior.
There's good and bad in every race,
Don't judge based on someone's face.
Treat everyone with respect and grace.
Learn this lesson, change your mind.
Remember we're all humankind.

**Black in White**

**Poems by Charlotte Shyllon**

## WE'RE IN SAINT LUCIA, AREN'T WE?

*By Charlotte Shyllon*

Eager to escape the cold and gloom,
We jumped at the chance to get away.
Happily, we walked into our hotel room
In a resort in Saint Lucia called Robin Bay.

It was a fourth floor room, luxurious and large
With amazing views of the bright blue sea.
We were here to relax, refresh, recharge
What an awesome place for us to be!

But then we saw it… the picture on the wall
Above the bed where we would sleep.
We were aghast, stunned at the gall.
In a Caribbean nation, the message was deep.

Here, where there's a majority Black population,
A photo of a White woman's feet on a beach
Spoke volumes about the expectation
That the hotel was out of Black people's reach.

But wait. Maybe we were mistaken;
Maybe it was just about diversity.
Maybe the image was simply taken
To show a different ethnicity.

## Black in White

But no. In a room along the corridor
Our family members faced a similar image.
And downstairs too, by the restaurant door,
It was Whiteness to which we had to pay homage.

Sure, there was local art in a few places.
But clearly the really prominent spots
Were reserved to showcase paler faces,
Catering for those arriving on yachts.

In hotels, what tends to be the norm
Is wall art that's neutral or even abstract;
Those in charge know why, and conform
To avoid upsetting guests, by lacking tact.

But it seems this hotel brand didn't dream
That it might be dicey in their accommodation
To use images that could make them seem
At best naive in this location.

We didn't let it spoil our vacation
But decided to share our expectation
That a hotel in a majority Black nation
Should consider this in the decoration.

It's not too much to ask…

# Poems by Charlotte Shyllon

## Quotable Quotes

"True belonging only happens when we present our authentic, imperfect selves to the world. Our sense of belonging can never be greater than our level of self-acceptance."

*Brene Brown*

**Black in White**

## STOP LUMPING US TOGETHER

*By Charlotte Shyllon*


If you've not already done so
It's time to abandon
Those catch-all phrases
Like BAME and BME
And definitely coloured!
For some, even the term
People of colour
May be problematic.

Lumping us all together
Simply diminishes
The diversity and richness of
Very different people.

Another thing…
When talking about Africa
Remember it is a CONTINENT,
Not one homogenous country.
Africa has more countries
Than any other continent.
That's 54 individual nations,
and over 1.4 billion people.

Lumping us all together
Simply diminishes
The diversity and richness of
Very different people.

Another thing…
People considered 'ethnic minorities'
Are a minority only in a Western context.
Collectively, that same grouping of people
Comprises around 85 percent
Of the world's population,
Making them instead
The 'Global Majority'.

The connotations
And implications
Of being in the Majority
Versus being a minority
Are empowering
And elevating.

Consider that when
Lumping us all together,
And stop it!

# SECTION 3:

# Guest Poets' Poems

# Black in White

## "I'M A NEW HIRE..."

*By PoetryGirl4.0*

I turn up, looking neat,
crisp tones in my voice,
LK Bennett shoes on my feet.
Everyone is greeted with a smile,
before they retreat,
except me!
A scowl meets me as if to say
how dare I appear,
at this interview,
as if I belong there!
"Who are you here to see?
If you are here for housekeeping,
the entrance is over there!"
My smile turns into a frown,
as her eyebrows rise higher.
"Good afternoon, I have a meeting
with Mr Jordan Banks Jnr at 2:30,
I'm a new hire".
Her mouth opened wide in disbelief,
Mr Banks is her boss
and she understood what that means...
that I'll be her boss soon too!
Her wide-open mouth,
in those few seconds said,
how did you get a job like this,
and it should really be my job instead!
"Please take a seat",
she said as she smiled sweetly,
continuing to say,

"he'll be right with you!"
I nod, and I say nothing as I retreat.
Seconds later, I'm hugged
as I'm greeted by Mr "Jordan Banks" Jnr,
the youngest CEO ever,
and from whom I'm taking over.
"Janet, be good to this young lady right here,
if you think I'm amazing,
she's a real pioneer.
The youngest and only black woman
to ever be in charge around here".
I smile, as I reply, "Oh, Jordan, that's so sweet!
Janet and I will get on just fine,
in fact, we already do,
don't worry, it'll be neat!"
Janet looked embarrassed,
as her eyes pleaded with mine.
Thank you, she mouthed.
This time, I smiled.
Ultimately, the power is mine.
I have faith in my abilities,
and it will all be fine!
The youngest and only black woman
to ever be in charge around here…

*PoetryGirl4.0 is the pen name of the poet who won the 2nd prize in the Black in White Poetry Competition 2021. Message her via the Black in White team at: info@blackinwhiteservices.co.uk.*

## Quotable Quotes

"The difference between equity and equality is that equality is when everyone gets the same thing, and equity is when everyone gets the things they deserve."

*DeRay Mckesson*

**Black in White**

## THIEF OR CLEANER, CLEANER OR THIEF?
*By PoetryGirl4.0*

What if I said that there are two schools of thought
when someone that looks like me
walks into a shop or office block?
In a shop, we're shadowed overtly.
"Just doing my job.
If you've got nothing to hide, why do you mind?"
These words aren't spoken of course,
it's in the look in the eyes and I can only surmise,
as I bump into the "security guard" for the tenth time.
I don't apologise, I wait for an explanation.
No use as it's obvious what that will be.
I walked in, well dressed, and looking fine,
but all he could see in me,
was a potential shoplifter,
a potential "tea leaf" or thief!
No matter that I'm hardworking, honest,
and what I earn in a day,
could feed him for at least the month of May.
No more to be said, no more to say...
I head into the office, armed with my lunch,
it's early, it's empty and I have a hunch
that I'll get in and get things done a plenty.
"Excuse me", I pause and start to turn,
"only executives are allowed through here",
I've turned now,
but thinking he must be challenging somebody else.
Worse yet, I know his name is Warren
and we talked on the way out last night.
"If you're with the cleaning company,

you can't come through here".
My mouth dropped, I was in shock.
Nothing wrong with being a cleaner
but I wouldn't be doing it in this frock.
I wondered whether I'd wandered into the twilight zone.
I pull out my ID badge and wave it Warren's way,
"you're joking, right" is all that I can say...
What a start to my day,
in less than an hour,
I've been challenged
first as a potential thief, then as a cleaner,
who doesn't know the score.
How about you challenge your thinking instead?
So, next time you see someone that looks like me,
that thief or that cleaner you think you see,
take it from me,
may not be who you think them to be!

## Quotable Quotes

"We all should know that diversity makes for a rich tapestry, and we must understand that all the threads of the tapestry are equal in value no matter what their colour."

*Maya Angelou*

## Black in White

# GIVE US OUR COUNTRY BACK...

*By PoetryGirl4.0*

"Give us our country back!
We're doing it for our children!
Stop the boats; burn the hotels...."

When did we all stop being human?
Does anyone really think that because horrifying things
were done to us in the past,
that those same things are okay today?
Let me just say "Heck no, no way"!

You work hard, help your community, make the world a better place,
and today you find that hate isn't blind,
but is blind to the journey you've walked in that skin,
to who you are and where you've been,
to all you've done and what you've seen and just like that,
in the blink of an eye…

You're attacked, your car burnt, a car is backed into your house,
where you travel from or to becomes a colour thing,
"If they're white, let them pass!"

For now, no more riots, but the hate is still bubbling
and even though there is now quiet,
still those hateful thoughts run riot…

More worrying is the number of children that were taken along
and exposed and encouraged to think
that treating someone as though they are less,
is not wrong and is the right view to express!

And, the thing is, if the haters go to ancestry.com,
they might discover that they're not as white as they think!

Give us our country back?
Hold on one second…
whose country is it anyway?

**Guest Poets' Poems**

## Quotable Quotes

"Diversity doesn't look like anyone. It looks like everyone."

*Karen Draper*

# Black in White

# FILTERS
*Serena Malcolm*

This child he has no filter,
Says exactly what he likes,
Utters every wicked insult
that his fledgling mind can write.

This child she has no filter,
So the peers that she maligns
(while baring milk teeth to the world)
are left reeling from the bile.

These children have no filters,
Yes, by nature, their tongues are loose,
But it's by nurture that they use them
to tie noose after verbal noose.

These children have no filters,
But they are filters, make no mistake,
Taught to think how Daddy thinks,
Taught to hate how Mummy hates.

They are filters with no filters,
Their good wolves left to starve
while their parents feed the bad ones
and hostile legacies are carved.

+++

*Author's note:*

*"It demands great spiritual resilience not to hate the hater whose foot is on your neck, and an even greater miracle of perception and charity not to teach your child to hate." James Baldwin*

*Serena Malcolm has been writing poetry for over three decades. Her poem 'Foreign Body' won 1st prize in the 2021 Black in White Poetry Competition. She is a member of the Black in White team.*
**Instagram: @serena_malcolm**

# Guest Poets' Poems

## Quotable Quotes

"I can tell you, without diversity, creativity remains stagnant."

*Edward Enninful*

**Black in White**

# IN THE SILENCE THAT IS MY RIGHT
*By Rick Dove*

Naive to mistake composure for ease,
Voluntary muscles can still be held still,
even as roiling blood rebels, even as
proud flesh is remembering its history,
birthright and etymologies, scarring
these flinching lynch pins remembering,
that The police protect property, not people,
making ownership the means of production,
remembering that they compensated slave
owner families on the abolition of slavery,
paid their descendants reparations until 2015,
(So, I was paying them for owning my family)
Naive to mistake composure for ease.

And the police protect property, uphold
the laws of our society, the system seethes,
as blind justice cannot see beyond its own
corruption. Here, ownership is the means
of production, land owned is land seized.
Borders and fences need to be defended.
And the police protect property not people,
Not the involuntary muscle this society still needs
to bleed, to feed the earth, for food to eat,
And I am paying them for caging me,
Naive to mistake this composure for ease.

## Black in White

And since the dawn of society, it has been
echoing on repeat, spiralling scaling symmetries,
they compensated slave owner families
on the abolition of slavery. And the police
protect property not people like me,
A total war of ideologies echoing on repeat
between those who'd exert control, and those
who would be free, finally freed,
Naive to mistake our composure for ease,
For in roiling blood is a raging sea,
And so many world-ending floods
in prophecies, So, I ask you again,
"Under what powers are you stopping me?"

*Rick Dove is a black, queer and disabled writer and activist from London. Widely anthologised since 2016, Rick became National Poetry Slam Champion in 2021, and has published two solo collections with Burning Eye Books.*
**Instagram, Threads, BlueSky: @rickdove**

# SECTION 4:

# Winning Poems 2024 – Workplace Category

**Black in White**

## Winning Poems

**1ST PRIZE**

## THE GIRL FROM NIUE: LUNCHBREAK AT PEGWORTH PLASTICS

*By John Gallas*

We sat in the shelter outside and gobbled our chips.
They gave me advice. They gave me some hooky tips.

What do you do when the tide comes in, they said.
*O pull up the ladder, lie down, and pretend we're dead.*

They watched things on YouTube. Talked to their phones. And laughed.
They mostly looked somewhere else. They thought I was daft.

Are there roads, they said. Drinking their Coke. And cars.
*O we ride on tigers mostly, and go by the stars.*

They looked at me sideways. They worried it might not be true.
O civilised tribe, come on: would I lie to you?

**Black in White**

**Winning Poems**

**2ND PRIZE**

# NOT ONE OF US!

*By Chantel Ndubuka*

New black female teacher
In a mainly white school.
It's not rocket science, love!
You're not one of us!

Some white teachers hostile;
Cloak and dagger experiences;
Secretive whispers because
You're not one of us!

Some white parents prejudiced;
Confirmed by other black staff.
They sent us a clear message that
You're not one of us!

Stepped into a classroom and
Students laughed at my surname.
Diluted top-down response because
You're not one of us!

Threatened twice in white school
By two male students.
Poor support from leaders because
You're not one of us!

Police informed of threats.
Shockingly dismissive approach!
Could it possibly be because
You're not one of us?

Determined to make an impact.
Resilience is one of my strengths!
But this was unwelcomed because
You're not one of us!

So, I left with great sadness.
So much value unexplored!
Still, the memory lingers that
You're not one of us!

## Quotable Quotes

"The path to diversity begins with supporting, mentoring, and sponsoring diverse women and men to become leaders and entrepreneurs."

*Denise Morrison*

# Black in White

**Winning Poems**

**3ʳᴰ PRIZE**

# UNHEARD

*By Andre Le Coz*

I wear the skin of ancestors' grief,
In a world that was never meant for me,
Endless echoes of the past beneath,
Colour lines that wound so deeply.

From classroom whispers to job-site glares,
Microaggressions that strip me bare,
I fight for space, I fight for air,
In this never-ending snare.

In the classrooms of my youth, their laughter stung
Words like knives, invisible but sharply wrung,
Lost in books but found in looks, I'd often hung,
A dream deferred by the songs that were never sung.

In boardrooms full of suits, they speak in coded tongue,
Their eyes avoid my own, as if my worth is none,
I bear the weight of history, a burden passed down long,
Stride forward in defiance, my spirit standing strong.

Each handshake feels a test, a challenge to my place,
A spotlight burns upon me in this predominantly white space,
Behind their cordial smiles, suspicion deeply sown,
Yet here I stand, persevering, making this place my own.

## Quotable Quotes

"Diversity is the one true thing we all have in common. Celebrate it every day."

*Winston Churchill*

# SECTION 5:

# Winning Poems 2024 – Childhood Category

# Black in White

> Winning Poems

> 1ST PRIZE

# THE REASON I PUNCHED GARY

*By Emma Conally-Barklem*

After Emily Zobel Marshall's 'The Reason I slapped Barry' in *Bath of Herbs*

We'd sat next to his carved mahogany ashtray, its proud curves like a totem pole spiralling Babel-like higher than my Jaki Graham topknot. We'd watched an old film, I'd cried without understanding the anguish of the brown girl who screamed, "Why can't I just be me!"

I'd felt that dissonance already at 7 without knowing what it was.

All this time he'd watched my confusion, then a nod as he said, "Raise your hands". I did automatically as if taken hostage. A flick of ash from his cig, and smile, "No, in fists".

He taught me how to punch, harder than I thought I should, soft knuckles hit grey wire smelling callouses still lined with an inside wall's dust. Flashed papercut sting from the unyield of him.

"Harder!" I hit with all the fury of the girl in the film, her tea-skin concealed in sepia like a pre-colour *Black and White Minstrel Show*. "Again!" "Faster!"

My wrists hurt; when he was satisfied I could attack when required to do so I soothed my mind by combing the blonde- haired blue- eyed *Girls World* doll's hair, its fine acrylic tresses knotted under tasselled *Care Bears* lightshade, and packed my bag for swim class.

"N****r, I'm gonna rape you!"

## Black in White

Next day, my mouth an 'O' filled with chlorine. Gary Walton's eyes slanted, fox-ginger hair in Terry Wogan style, venom picked through metered water. I didn't understand but knew the words were bad. I thought of sugar cane and Lumb Lane and grave unchartered waters.

Hands made the shape he'd coached into violence. *Bop!* Gary fell back like an extra in a Bruce Lee movie, ginger met chemical soup, a red spout, an angry whale's gush as he *did* bleed.

I thought of dad and my Jamaican grandma Rosa's purple string shopping bag. Silent grandad Louis tending chickens tendered by warm lamp.

And stayed home at the school's request, my mind swimming cap blank, laid on my eiderdown bed,

and read.

## Quotable Quotes

"We need to reach that happy stage of our development when differences and diversity are not seen as sources of division and distrust, but of strength and inspiration."

*Josefa Iloilo*

**Black in White**

**2ND PRIZE**

# MY SKIN IS MADE OF EARTH

*By Gwyn Yvere*

Dirt.
Wet, muddy Earth.
"Black," the young girl spewed,
Her face the colour of my palms.
She cursed the word the only way she knew how.
Like venom on hot tar.
Her parents taught her well.

I didn't need to know she "wasn't allowed" to talk to me,
but the bigotry bubbling in her
bones was second nature.
I didn't hate her for her ignorance,
But as I looked in the mirror,
I found Prejudice had already started
sprouting from my skin.

**Black in White**

**Winning Poems**

**3RD PRIZE**

# A PUPPET OF YOUR PARENTS
*By Yohana Gasu (Age 17)*

Have you ever looked at my deep, brown eyes and thought
"My boundless, blue pools are better than his?"
Have you ever gazed at the plumpness of my lips and thought to yourself
"They'd be better if they were thin."?
Have you ever glared at the skin that I wear and thought
"That's too much melanin? It is better to be fair in complexion."?
No, for no child should have such thoughts.
My darling if your brain has forged such routes, perhaps it was never really yours to begin with?

In the womb, you have yet to look into the eyes of another.
In the warmth, you do not gaze at any lips, not even your own.
In the darkness, there was no 'fair', nor 'melanin' to glare at.
So, dear little one, who taught your eyes to look, to gaze, to glare with such contempt?

Who led your finger to point with such conviction?
Who chose the peach crayon to be your favourite and the brown to be inadequate?
Who painted the perception in your mind that it was right to be nice but only to people of 'your kind'?
Who established that you were to have a kind rather than to be it?
Who fed you the words 'weird' and 'strange', but led you to believe to be different was deserving of hatred?
Who taught your little mouth to sow such poison, but did not tell you those weeds would harm you as much as 'them'?
Who taught you that there was even a 'them' to begin with?

Who taught you, my darling?

Have you looked at the strings tethered to your limbs?
Have you gazed at the sticks hovering above your head?
Now, turn and glare at they who taught you those things?
Who do you see? Do you see them?

Now, release those fetters,
Break those chains,
Cut those ties
You are free to look at my eyes and yours and see they both have beauty,
To gaze at my lips and yours and feel not jealousy but amazement.
You may glare, not at me or yourself, but my darling glare at Injustice and pity her;
For she too had a mother and a father
Who saw her as a puppet rather than a daughter.

# SECTION 6:

# Highly Commended Poems 2024

### in alphabetical order by poem title

## A CASE OF MISTAKEN IDENTITY?

*By Yvette Beckley*

**CATEGORY: WORKPLACE**

On the phone
I speak
with the doctor.
Providing information
about the patient

Yes,
please attend
the case conference.
Your input
is vital.

I knock at the door
The red bow -tied
Consultant
sees me
You.......
Must be the carer

No,
I'm the manager
Oh!
He smiles

You're welcome
I say in my mind
to the non-existent
apology.

I give my invaluable input.

**Highly Commended Poems**

CATEGORY: CHILDHOOD

# A JOURNEY THROUGH JUDGEMENT

*By Jamal Adewunmi (Age 14)*

In the glow of youth's innocent dawn,
I trod upon paths where shadows spawn,
In the gentle winds of early years' grace,
I felt the sting of a world's embrace.

Skin kissed by sun, yet marked by shade,
Invisible chains where freedom should wade,
Through laughter's dance and playground's glee,
Lurked whispers sharp as thorns on tree.

In classrooms bright with learning's light,
I found myself a solitary sight,
Where textbooks spoke of a world so fair,
But reality whispered a different air.

Their eyes would linger, their whispers sly,
As if my hue was a reason to decry,
My heart still pure, my dreams ablaze,
But shackled by judgments in hidden ways.

Oh, how I yearned for equality's song,
To drown out the echoes of prejudice strong,
To walk hand in hand, side by side,
With hearts that saw beyond skin's divide.

## Black in White

Yet through the pain, a strength did rise,
A flame within, a steadfast prize,
For in the crucible of adversity's test,
I found resilience, a spirit blessed.

So let them judge by beauty's grace,
And measure words in this poetic space,
For my tale speaks not just of woe,
But of courage, resilience, and dreams that grow.

In the tapestry of life's grand design,
Let my voice echo, let it shine,
For though racism's trials may leave their scar,
They cannot dim the light of who we are.

## Highly Commended Poems

**CATEGORY: WORKPLACE**

# AN EDUCATED BLACK MAN SIGNING ON IN 21ST CENTURY BRITAIN
*By Dr G*

Why does this still persist?
Despite extensive education, if Black, bias still exists
If a man, even worse employers often still resist
Black man and education treated regularly as a dichotomy

Going to sign-on, you see my education
The main emotion I'm feeling is one of frustration
Job Centre deaf when employers don't want educated Black men, my situation
If I were that good, I wouldn't be here so told

When I mention stats of significant racial disparity, I'm pulling the race card
Wish I could laugh with irony, but my stomach is growling as I starve
Let's talk about jobs available with my education a mile and a yard
But you insist on me applying for a warehouse job

Who is pulling the race card when you ignore quality I possess?
Why because I'm a Black man, only using hands is my subject?
I talk about what I've done and can do, but your sights I object
Insistence on the lowest rung because you've racialised me to be low

I'm an educated Black man needing benefits
Told play down my qualifications, or a job I can't get into it
If I can't be accepted as me, then I'll never in work fit
Sign of societal bigotry I will not succumb

## Black in White

Why do you have an attitude? so I was told
Wouldn't anyone when faced with hostility open and bold
When confronted, notes of opinions kept, not facts, when records were to unfold
Ignored plethora of jobs applied for that they knew

I'm an educated Black man looking for work
Being calm when ignored and attacked when you would have gone berserk
In seeking opportunities, I never shirked
If you have ten chances, I'm lucky to find one

Why do you have an attitude? so I was told
Actually more like why because I'm an educated Black man with skills undersold
I'm losing, but I'll eventually win, smile on my face you'll see will be bold
When I find an employer that values my worth

## Highly Commended Poems

**CATEGORY: WORKPLACE**

# BEING A WOMAN OF COLOUR IN POLICING
*By Saara Nawaz*

So, what does it mean to be a woman of colour police officer in today's day and age?
For me, my values align intrinsically, It's much more than just a wage,

And no, I'm not forced to wear my Hijab, nor am I oppressed,
There is so much more to me, than the way that I am dressed.

We are not like the negative media perceptions, we are more than just a tick box,
We have more in common than divides us, like the saying of the late Jo Cox,

Some may not like differences, and despise dissimilarity,
They say we don't belong here. We don't contribute to society.

Well, my grandfather was in the British army, he fought in World War Two,
He risked his life for a country where he didn't grow up nor knew,

He did it to help save lives, putting others before his own needs,
Because our values teach us that saving a life Is one of the greatest of deeds,

Now that is the ultimate sacrifice, which instilled in me this passion,
To strive, to serve, to protect, with determination and compassion,

What makes some of us different, are the things you may critique,
But this is what makes us all beautiful, it's what makes us all unique,

It is not enough to say I'm not racist, see, you must be anti-racist too,
This means to proactively tackle discrimination, which is the responsibility of both me and you,

Like Ani DiFranco said, "there is strength in the differences between us, there is comfort where we overlap."
So, let's take these disparities seriously, and do more to close the gap,

To ensure we all support our colleagues in bringing their authentic self to work,
To stamp out unfair treatment is an obligation we simply cannot shirk,

Now you may not be a person of colour, not black nor Asian but white,
But you have an imperative part to play, to help challenge and change the wrongs to right,

So, let's better understand these challenges that are perpetuated in every race report,
And implement the steps to inclusivity and provide the necessary support,

So, let's take the steps towards equality no matter how big or small,
Because to be more inclusive, diverse and representative, is a place that works for all!

**Highly Commended Poems**

CATEGORY: CHILDHOOD

# BETWEEN THE ROCK AND THE WALL
*By Carole Greco*

The sign stood awkwardly in the walkway, at an angle,
Like it was sorry to be there,
Black letters against peeling, sun-bleached wood.
'Whites Only'.

Eight-year-old me swims in the tidal pool
Green-tinged water all around,
Shimmering and quivering in the way that water does
With its heavy, jelly body.

The little boy comes to stand on the whitewashed pool wall,
His skin, brown and warm and smooth in the sun.
He looks into the water and smiles to himself,
Seeming to imagine he is king of the sea.

I listen as the beach becomes silent,
The way it always does when he comes to swim.
The voices hush and become woven through
with whispers and threats and sounds of words I do not understand.
Only the gulls stir the stillness of the salty air
As they swirl overhead in lazy circles,
While I swim between the rock and the wall.

Years later, and the faded sign is gone now,
But I still wonder about the boy
And if he remembers the beach
And those salt-stained days where the silence became

As thick as a thing I could hold in my hand,
And where the girl swam
Between the rock and the wall.

+++

*Author's note: The sign was one of many across the beaches of my South African childhood in the 1980s. I learned sometime later that the boy was the son of a visiting diplomat and had immunity from the 'whites only beaches' rule.*

**Highly Commended Poems**

CATEGORY: CHILDHOOD

# BLACK GIRL, WHITE WORLD
*By Karenne Small*

Why does everyone stop and stare?
And point at my skin and my nose and my hair?
I try to pretend that I don't care
But it hurts

Why is everyone light skinned and I'm so dark?
And why does it make them all comment and laugh?
I attempt to ignore them but the pain's too sharp
And it hurts

Why am I so fat and they're so thin?
Mum says I look 'healthy' but it's hard to fit in
So I blink back my tears and paste on a fake grin
Yet it hurts

They say I smell funny and I try to explain;
It's cocoa-butter or hair oil – they hold their nose and complain
So I spend my days with my head hanging in shame
'Cos it hurts

They don't bother to whisper when they loudly compare
Their straight silky locks with my coarse frizzy hair
I pretend I can't hear them so they're not aware
That it hurts

They make me repeat things again and again
They mock my accent – because they say I sound 'foreign'
I sigh (inside I think I speak better than them)
Oh, it hurts

When they make monkey noises that are aimed at me
And ask "What's it like to swing in the trees?"
Or say "You should be grateful that we set you free"
God it hurts

For now, the best place that I can be
Is hidden inside books where I'm free to be me
Where characters are friends who accept me completely;
Where there's no hurt

**Highly Commended Poems**

CATEGORY: CHILDHOOD

# BUT HAVE *YOU* EVER EXPERIENCED RACISM?

*By Neelam Sharma*

My white sister-in-law asks me if I've ever experienced racism.

I think about the shouts of 'get out Paki',
to my fourteen-year-old sister
as she cycled her new bike down our road.

The dull thud of snowballs thrown at our windows
by boys who lived on the estate.
Our house alone a target.

The job my Dad lost when he raised a complaint
after finding out
he wasn't promoted because he's Asian.

The scrabbling for rent money in the eighteen months
he spent out of work, being told:
'I would hire you but my business partner won't have an Indian.'

The teachers who mocked me making sandwiches at school camp –
I was eleven, had made chapatis from scratch at home
but never sandwiches and was making enough for 100 students.

The teacher at choir auditions who told the class,
singing was more difficult for me,
confusing my fellow students who didn't know what he meant.
I knew.

# Black in White

The switching of a boy during a disagreement,
the shock of being called a 'f**king Paki!'
by someone I fancied, wanted to be my boyfriend.

The time as a skinny fourteen-year-old out on my first shopping trip
with a friend,
when a punk put his hand round my neck,
laughing to his pals that he could squeeze the life from me,
on the streets of Cambridge.

Somehow the words don't come to explain this and more.

Yes, I tell her, I have experienced racism.

**Highly Commended Poems**

**CATEGORY: WORKPLACE**

# DARK CINDERELLA

*By Cristina Akos Obazee (Age 17)*

I often call my Mama "Dark Cinderella"
Because that's how those in power treat her.
Each day she struggles as she gets looked down like she was a mere mouse
Such a beautiful woman she is yet they add a line of wrinkles on her each day.
I swear it was everybody's job to keep everything clean and tidy
Until she came along and that's when they only saw her as a cleaner.
They dumped the pressure of five people on her as if she could handle it
As if once she breaks apart, then they could happily get more like her as a replacement.

Each night I hear her sorrows and prayers
As if the fairy godmother would help her with just a ballroom dress
The problem is not the dress. The problem isn't even related to a ball or party.
The problem in their eyes was God's heavenly gift on her. Her beautiful dark skin
Such skin which carries years of blood and old history was what they were against for
Would that same skin give her the happy ending she once wished for?
Or would those menacing tyrants attempt to take her happiness away and turn her into their own little robot?

At that point I wonder
Will she overpower that evil stepmother with a shiny slipper?
Or will she use her roaring voice
A voice which carries those who are in the same path as her or worse,
And help us be freed from the tyrant yoke?

**Black in White**

> **CATEGORY: WORKPLACE**

# IFS, BUTS, AND MAYBES

*By Anu Kehinde*

The art is in the subtleties.

I love your hair.
You communicate so well.
Oh, you have a master's?
Your CV is so extensive.
You've done well for yourself.

Colleagues singing your praises but reminding you not to work too hard
(but you have to, just to be seen)
and of course, they love your ideas and creative flair
(but at least you're not just warming the chair)

Line managers hailing your talents in private,
yet taking credit in the guise of teamwork.
You agreed to this after all,
"able to work as a team" sitting on your resumé.
(Does wanting credit make you a jerk?)

(Maybe you seemed happy to be involved,
maybe you didn't seem hungry enough to want more for yourself,
maybe you should just be happy to be there.
they pay your bills after all.)

It's exhausting, being the property of the place you work.
Knowing you've come a long way but there is still more to learn...
More to learn about being black in a white space,
a reminder that you have to earn
your place.

There is more to learn about rejection from them
and the dejection that follows afterward.

Being the token quota.
Sitting like a trophy prize on the lowest shelf,
being the mutest voice,
being afraid of yourself,
of being othered, being wrong, being seen for the fraud you probably
are…

Always the oxymoron,
always the juxtaposition,
always the 'ifs', 'buts', and 'maybes'.

Maybe next time for the management role,
(next time never came.)
Maybe next time for the development course,
(next time never came.)
If only you could show us more of this skill in your current role,
(I've shown you all my cards and you took my ideas and ran with them.)
If only you could work better with more stakeholders,
(I'm liked by all because I remind myself to hold my mother's tongue,
to always be agreeable, never too loud, always humble.)

(Maybe if my efforts, twice as much as my counterparts, could be
noticed.)
(Maybe if I had been more outspoken?
Or louder?
Risked being the black stereotype…)

(Maybe) you would have been seen.
(Maybe) you wouldn't feel so stuck,
(Maybe) you wouldn't feel like you betrayed yourself.

### Black in White

If only I didn't feel so disappointed for changing,
being a chameleon to feel accepted.
If only I had chosen a line of work that didn't require masquerading.
If only I had chosen a space where blackness was represented.

If only I considered the maybes, there would be no buts.

## Highly Commended Poems

**CATEGORY: WORKPLACE**

# INTERVIEWING WHILST BLACK
*By Dr G*

More trauma than 9/11
Before you ask, I've been there
Gone on for decades, but still going
A situation most unfair

Interviewing whilst Black
Symptom of most common mental disorder in the street
Minimisation of maximum accomplishments consistent
To overcome is a monumental feat

We can't compete when jobs are non-compete
Filtered listening because the listeners are slack
Dead pan feedback delivery where truth is a mystery
Why the need for this attack?

When job success dependent
On whether the manager is comfortable with Black people
If not, game done, no matter what's said at interview
Feedback of fiction whilst it's said we're equal

This delusionality symptom most existent
When jobs go unfilled rather than hiring Black
Tears shed, confidence lost, pride reeketh away
These still too often 21st century facts

We can prepare, our experience and skills we share
But cannot win when ocular-audial deficiencies prevent interviewers from listening

Record perceptions of negativity, don't hear our positivity
Constant experiences keep our tears glistening

Interviewing whilst Black
There no defence against this attack
Because the perpetrators hold all the evidence
When questioned, they double down successfully whilst we unreasonably fall flat

How do we solve the problem?
When we're gas lit and suppressed from delving into the question
Interviewing whilst Black, most socially accepted form of quiet attack
Symptom of societal anti-Black oppression

**Highly Commended Poems**

**CATEGORY: WORKPLACE**

# INVISIBLE CHAINS ON ME
*By Paarth Aggarwal (under 18)*

In the office where ambition flows,
A hidden current, darkness shows.
Beneath the surface, unseen ties,
Invisible chains, silent lies.

Morning greetings, cordial masks,
Yet prejudice in mundane tasks.
A jest, a glance, a knowing smirk,
Cutting deeper, unseen work.

In meetings, my voice subdued,
Ideas dismissed, attitudes rude.
Promotion paths, just out of sight,
Talent dimmed by bias' blight.

Lunch breaks, isolated, cold,
Colleagues' laughter, tales retold.
Isolation, a heavy shroud,
Amongst the many, alone in the crowd.

Yet through the weight, my spirit fights,
Challenging the wrongful slights.
For though they bind, these chains unseen,
My heart remains forever keen.

Invisible chains may tether me,
But they can't shackle dreams set free.
With every step, I break their hold,
In unity, our strength unfolds.

**CATEGORY: WORKPLACE**

# MISSION

*By Mike Dixon*

I may be old, I may be white, but I'm no less up for the fight;
to make our sector as diverse as can be, and ensure there is true equal opportunity.
I grew up thinking all was fair, how could I have been so unaware?
My eyes now open I understand, to make a difference we need all hands.
It's not about black or white, it's about being together to maintain what's right.
Each of us has a role to play, to ensure unconscious prejudice does not get in the way.
It sounds so simple, but rarely is, we need to maintain the focus across our biz.
As individuals we can all play our part, if we have this mission within our heart.
Our goal is clear, for us to win, a world where our children only see the person within.

**Highly Commended Poems**

CATEGORY: CHILDHOOD

# NATURAL SELECTION
*By Izabella Osijo (Age 15)*

One random Tuesday, not long ago,
I went out to the playground for lunch.
Together with my friends, hand in hand,
Our cheeks hurt from laughing so much.

Soon after my laughter was cut short,
With a hard THUMP to the back of my head.
I pushed my face into a smile, hiding tears,
Frustration building at the football boys ahead.

'Sorry my bad', one of them shouted,
Eager to return to their game.
'Don't apologise to her', another muttered,
But I ignored him all the same.

I went to catch up with friends,
Until the same boy yelled my name across the pitch of concrete,
This time followed by another name,
One I'd never heard until that week.

His lips started to curl as he spoke,
An N morphing through a hard g and soft r,
My eyebrows furrowed as I watched him start to laugh,
Like a hyena as it goes for the kill.

One random Tuesday,
I learnt that only one word could define the history of millions of tortured souls,

**Black in White**

On a random weekday, at some point in my childhood,
A boy's words inspired me to take a stand and help my people's history be understood.

**Highly Commended Poems**

**CATEGORY: WORKPLACE**

# SMALL WOUND

*By Isaura Barbé-Brown*

She lay bleeding from her head.
A bruise rising on her cheek from
where he struck her.
The wound just behind her ear from the
curb she fell against.

She lay weeping.
Her feet stretched out
into the centre of the road
in danger of oncoming traffic.

We'd heard the commotion.
The fight.
We'd rushed outside.
Some had chased her lover.
Her attacker.
I rushed to her.

I feared for her broken head.
I feared for her breaking heart.
As gently as I could I held her head
in my lap.

I pressed a clean cloth to her head.
I said softly…
Do not worry.
Help is coming.
You are safe.

## Black in White

She tilted her bleeding head up
and turned her wet eyes towards me
for the first time
and I felt her body shudder
and her top lip curled up
in spite
in hate and she said

Get your fucking hands off me you dirty black bitch.

And I felt the venom of a
viper who would have struck
if she had been able.

As gently as I came
I placed her head back on the tarmac.
I got off my knees and I turned around
and I went back in.

I washed her blood from my hands.
I went back behind the bar.
I poured a drink.

I heard the ambulance arrive
but I did not turn to see the lights.

**Highly Commended Poems**

CATEGORY: CHILDHOOD

# SO WHY AREN'T WE PLEASED BY THE TOKEN BLACK POET?

*By Ross Clarke*

There's something in the tone of voice he used
When telling her she 'isn't in our group',
Or maybe in other unsubtle clues –
She might be young, but I know she's not duped.

And when I get his mother on the phone
It's clear that I'm swimming against the tide,
That racist child is scummy mummy's clone,
Apparently it's me who called to lie.

Then when I see two classmates getting on,
Their friendship becomes tense when he's around,
I see them hold their breath until he's gone,
At once it is both nothing and profound.

I watch as other teachers assign sports
To children who'd rather be reading
Or watching and cheering their classmates on courts,
Not in front of the whole classroom pleading.

And in assembly to receive awards
I see the children cringe to hear their name,
Sinking towards an old man, plus clipboard,
Bestowing mispronunciation blame.

So why aren't we pleased by the token black poet?
Why must month-long celebrations insult?
Why must we raise our babies to know it
Will not just come from children but adults?

**Black in White**

> **CATEGORY: CHILDHOOD**

## STILL LIVING

*By Mbeke Waseme*

I was 11
You should have known better
Introducing yourself
With 'I've never taught
Black children before'
We looked at you with
more suspicion than you'll
ever know
Yet, with your power
You would serve the final blow.

Where did you copy
that poem from?
Bring me the book,
and I'll be light on you.
I didn't copy
it miss
I didn't copy it
Miss
But you would not hear.
All congested with
Your fear
I diiiiiidn't
Copy it
Miss!
Yet you kept me back
I could not show you
the book that

Didn't exist,
The book you
Insisted
I had copied from.

I sat looking
at you
With all
your fear,
the fear
That ensured
You just couldn't hear
You would not hear
That I was a writer
and great.
An 11-year-old
Black girl
That shouldn't have
Existed
in your world.

I didn't
(One slap)
Copy it!
(Two slaps)
Miss!
(Three slaps)
I was not going down
I was just gonna
Keep coming back.

You never
gave up
And I never

gave in.
And the racism
That blinded you
Is the
World
I am still in


+++

*Author's note:*
*This happened when I was 11 years old; I am now 59 and still living in that world*

**Highly Commended Poems**

**CATEGORY: WORKPLACE**

# TAKE IT WHERE?!

*By Niam Moore*

*My first job ever lasted just under four weeks*
*Knocking doors… many stayed closed, the rest I didn't reach*
*One door, his door*
*I'm still paying rent for…*

[Knock, Knock]

"Don't worry, I'm not as bad as I look"
Rehearsed words freed from full lips finally not facing doors closed

Countenance contorts
Mouth agape
Eyebrows lower
Cruel words emanate

Stood blankly in my tabard fundraising for the deaf
No one should ever have to hear what was said on that front step

I chuckle at the absurdity
        Or
To stop myself from screaming

They say it's not as bad as it's been
But sorry if I'm not believing

Words understood yet asinine, nonsensical
Come from a closed mind aged but inflexible
Correct in grammar, prosody and syntax

### Black in White

It's not even the meaning I struggle to catch
It's temerity, the flippancy of which it was spoken
As if prattling off facts, edicts, or cosy held notions

Brazen, brash, bald-faced, blatant
Whittled down my character to one single, foolish statement
One look at me and you'd decided my worth
Young.
        Black.
                Boys.
Only deserve to be hurt
Instead of hearing my words you made your own words weapons
You missed all my traits, you deduced me in seconds

Self-aware. Patient. Empathetic.
Caring. Kind. Razor-sharp wit.

Nephew. Cousin. Friend. Son.
English. Jamaican. Barbadian.

Missed all my traits, deduced me in seconds
Instead of hearing my words you made your own words weapons
Maybe I don't have the words to otherwise convince
So your audacity will stay paired with your ignorance

I asked for a donation
But you volunteered something else
A pin to burst my bubble
Show me the ills of this world

I chuckle at the absurdity
        Or
To stop myself from screaming.

## Highly Commended Poems

Silent alarm rings in my shock
Warned since birth yet still I forgot
Words understood remain nonsensical
But if I'd responded in kind *my* actions would be Indefensible
Reprehensible a slave to systemic double standards
So, I hold my tongue and refrain from the candid

---

Sweat grooves in palms
Because to dance is in my culture
        Missteps
backwards.
        Missteps
                forwards.

Memories swirl unprovoked as I try to locate calm

Harmless but harmed from mouth with sharp tongue
I've heard words do not hurt
But these words had not come
The hurt was not physical
But these words were not gentle
And now I stand at this front door untying knots in my mental

    Because.

I resent myself
I resent that I feel like this
I resent that I can be made to feel like this
I resent that I can be made to feel like this by someone, anyone
I resent that I can be made to feel like this because of the colour of my skin

### Black in White

In this moment, shockingly, I do not even resent him


I resent feeling torn about telling my mum
I resent futures for children that are yet to come
I resent failings in education
I resent no changes in education
I resent corporations whose actions show compliance
Stirring up confidence for the minority to break silence

I resent flat out denial
I resent turning the other cheek
I resent unwillingness to accept
I resent knowing this will repeat

I resent that I cannot grow large
And bang at your closing door
My giant voice bellowing
I WON'T TAKE THIS NO MORE!

      Instead.

Like too many before who silently got on
I left trying to figure out what **I** had done wrong.

**Highly Commended Poems**

**CATEGORY: CHILDHOOD**

# THEY KNOW TOO

By *Nicole Kasumu*

I knew I was black,
But, that day. I KNEW I WAS BLACK.

I just wanted to play,
1,2,3, 4.
Ok, so I get 1,2,3, ew
No…. you can't be a cop,
You're black, you have to be a baddie!

I cried.
I laugh now, if only life was still that plain, simple, ignorant.
Funniest part,
It came from a brother, not even two shades lighter.

I knew I was black,
My parents Nigerian,
We spoke Yoruba and Ibibio at home.
But that was the first time I realised, everyone else knew too.

I don't have the same nose,
But neither does Rachel.
It's different with shade though.
With hair or nose or eyes or fingers,
They're all different, but share the same functions, expectations.
But with shade, I'm a baddie and if ever so slightly lighter, I'm good?
They thought that.
S**t! Did my teachers?
Were they secretly expecting me to fail,

### Black in White

With the decorum to keep it to themselves.

Maybe if I change my elocution,
Lose my language,
'act like them', as though I had been acting any different up until that point.
Maybe I'll be good,
Seen as good.
Though you can't hide from the darkness in your shade.

Now it's a lot more subtle,
I somewhat miss the blatant brutally.
It easier to fight a brother not even two shades lighter, when he Spits in your face,
than it is Calmly react to a back-handed compliment about the colour of my extensions or texture of my 'fro.

I knew I was black,
Now, even more so.
But I pray that being other, different, Bad, Black,
aren't the defining features of that.
Only time will tell.

**Highly Commended Poems**

**CATEGORY: CHILDHOOD**

# TRUE COLOURS

*By JoshuaF (Age 11)*

My colours shine brighter than
the sun, bright enough
for everyone
just to laugh and bring me down
My tears fall like rain
I am laughed at again
These racists are driving me
insane.
My life feels so lame as
I walk down the path of shame

I need a heater and a coat as their ice-cold shards as sharp as a knife stab me.

But there are better things in life and now that I understand and now those shards don't do a thing to me anymore.

I don't care about what they say.

I let my true colours shine through, any way…

> CATEGORY: CHILDHOOD

## WHAT'S IN A NAME?

*By Eltayeb Bashar*

What's in a name?
It's messy introductions,
It's "What kind of name is that,
Can I call you something else?"
My name is we love multiculturalism
But the most I can do is a "Mohamed"

What's in a name?
It's the repetition of a broken record,
To say my name so many times
That it sounds foreign on my own lips,
My name is a lecture,
My name is a UN peacekeeping mission

What's in a name?
It's the joke of the classroom,
Its the snigger at the class register,
It's teachers, butchering your name
And demanding that you "take it or leave it"
My name is red lines and autocorrect,
My name is an immortal enemy of Microsoft Word

So what's in a name?
It's my ancestors washing in the Nile,
It is the fall of empires under African sunsets.
It's the migration from north to west,
And the miracle of my birth in Europe
My name is the birth of Africa in my heart,
My name is a borderless nation,
My name is the pain of the indigenous,
And the hope of all immigrants,
My name is a life raft
and dead children on front pages,
My name is faith in tomorrow
when you can't see anything today

# WHO AM I?

*By Theone Ampofo (Age 15)*

**CATEGORY: CHILDHOOD**

Black.

I believe that I am black and I am beautiful.
That's what my mum told me anyway.
That's not what the people at school say though.
The accusing stares when I get a new hairstyle,
The small glances in my direction at the slight mention of another black person.
The list goes on really.

I believe that I am black and I am beautiful.
That's what my mum told me anyway.
That's not what social media says though.
White, Blonde hair, Blue eyes, button nose
But I'm black and I'm still beautiful. Right?

I believe that I am black and I am beautiful.
That's what my mum told me anyway.
That's not what the world says though.
Thugs, Angry black women, Thieves, gang members.
I believe that I am black and I am beautiful.
But why does nobody else?

Why am I followed in stores?
Why am I judged by my name?
Why am I mocked and laughed at for my accent?
Why am I denied the same treatment as everyone else?
Why am I black?

But it doesn't matter why
It only matters who.
I believe that I am black and I am beautiful.
That is what my mum taught me.

## Quotable Quotes

"A diverse mix of voices leads to better discussions, decisions, and outcomes for everyone."

*Sundar Pichai*

# SECTION 7:

# About Black in White

## About Us

Black in White began in late 2020 following the publication of an eponymous book of poems that Charlotte Shyllon wrote about some of her experiences of racism in the workplace. She was motivated to write these poems following the murder of George Floyd in May 2020.

Like so many of us, Charlotte was deeply struck by how entrenched and endemic racist attitudes continue to result in such horrifying killings and the daily demeaning of Black people. She reflected on her experiences of racism – particularly while working in the corporate world for over 25 years where such things were rarely spoken about – and decided to tell some of her stories.

Black in White uses poetry to contribute to conversations around racism in the workplace and childhood. We seek to open minds and help put an end to racial inequality.

The Black in White Poetry Competition will continue to be run as a key programme under the auspices of The Transforming Words Foundation charity.

## Our Products

To date, five Black in White poetry books have been published with poems by Charlotte and over 130 contributing poets. The poems are about racism in the workplace and childhood, resulting from the annual Black in White Poetry Competition. The poems tell stories and share ideas and learnings to help make the corporate space, educational environments and society in general more inclusive.

There are also Black in White 4-page discussion guides, A4 posters and A5 postcards designed to help foster important dialogue in teams and for individuals around some of the key themes of equity, diversity and inclusion.

The Black in White books are available for purchase from most major online book retailers. The books and the rest of our product range (priced from £3.99 to £14.99 + postage & packaging) can also be obtained from: https://www.blackinwhiteservices.co.uk/store/

## Our Services

We'd love to hear from you if you are looking: 1) for a creative and engaging way to have conversations about racism in your workplace or in an educational setting; 2) to access our equity, diversity and inclusion consultancy or mentoring services; or 3) to enquire about bespoke projects or sponsorship opportunities. Charlotte is also available to participate in interviews, presentations, panel discussions and poetry readings.

## Our Team

The team comprises several amazing individuals who over the last one to four years have played a key role in helping to plan and implement the Black in White activities and initiatives.

Top row: **David, Hanna, Marcia**
Middle row: **Debbie, Charlotte, Sarah**
Bottom row: **Denyse, Jackie, Serena**

## Contact Us

The Black in White Poetry Competition will continue to be run as a key programme under the auspices of The Transforming Words Foundation charity.

To contact us please email charlotte@transformingwords.co.uk

www.ingramcontent.com/pod-product-compliance
Lightning Source LLC
Chambersburg PA
CBHW070542170426
43200CB00011B/2520